Bilingüe/
Bilingual

Caballos/Horses

Caballos cuarto de milla

American Quarter Horses

por/by Kim O'Brien

Editora consultora/Consulting Editor:
Gail Saunders-Smith, PhD

CAPSTONE PRESS
a capstone imprint

Pebble Books are published by Capstone Press,
1710 Roe Crest Drive, North Mankato, Minnesota 56003
www.capstonepub.com

Library of Congress Cataloging-in-Publication Data
O'Brien, Kim, 1960-
  [American quarter horses. Spanish & English]
  Caballos cuarto de milla = American quarter horses / por\by Kim
O'Brien.
      p. cm. — (Pebble bilingue/bilingual: cabollos/horses)
  Includes index.
  ISBN 978-1-4296-9224-3 (library binding)
  ISBN 978-1-62065-279-4 (ebook PDF)
  1. Quarter horse—Juvenile literature. I. Title. II. Title: American quarter horses.
SF293.Q3O2718 2013
636.1'33—dc23   2011051337

Summary: a brief introduction to the characteristics, life cycle, and uses of
the American quarter horse breed

Note to Parents and Teachers

The Caballos/Horses set supports national science standards
related to life science. This book describes and illustrates American
quarter horses. The images support early readers in understanding
the text. The repetition of words and phrases helps early readers
learn new words. This book also introduces early readers to subject
specific vocabulary words, which are defined in the Glossary
section. Early readers may need assistance to read some words and
to use the Table of Contents, Glossary, Internet Sites, and Index
sections of the book.

Printed in the United States of America in North Mankato, Minnesota.
042012   006682CGF12

Table of Contents

Tabla de contenidos

A Sprinting Horse

The American quarter horse
is a fast sprinter.
It runs faster
than other horse breeds
over a short distance.

Un caballo esprínter

El caballo cuarto de milla es un
esprínter muy veloz.
Corre una distancia corta más
rápido que cualquier otra
raza de caballo.

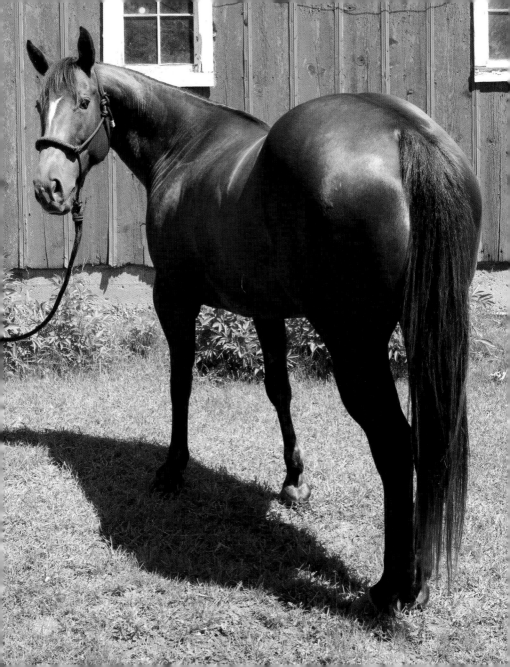

Quarter horses have muscular bodies. Strong hindquarters give the horses quick bursts of speed.

Los caballos cuarto de milla tienen un cuerpo musculoso. Las ancas fuertes dan impulsos rápidos de velocidad a los caballos.

sorrel
alazán
dun
pardo

8

Quarter horses' coats
can be one of many colors.
Sorrel, dun, and gray
are common coat colors.

El pelaje de los cuarto de milla
puede ser de muchos colores.
Alazán, pardo y gris son
colores comunes de pelaje.

From Foal to Adult

Female quarter horses give birth
to one foal at a time.
Newborn foals have
fuzzy coats and wobbly legs.

De potrillo a adulto

Las yeguas cuarto de milla dan
a luz a un potrillo por vez.
Los potrillos recién nacidos
tienen pelajes poco definidos
y patas inestables.

withers

cruz

In the United States, horses are measured in hands. In many other countries, they are measured in centimeters. Each hand is 4 inches (10 centimeters). A horse is measured from the ground to its withers.

En Estados Unidos, los caballos se miden en manos. En muchos otros países, se miden en centímetros. Cada mano mide 4 pulgadas (10 centímetros). Un caballo se mide desde el suelo hasta su cruz.

Quarter horses are fully grown after about four years. Adults stand 14.2 to 16 hands high.

Los caballos cuarto de milla se hacen adultos en unos cuatro años. Los adultos miden de 142 a 160 centímetros de alzada.

Riding and Rodeos

Quarter horses are calm. People like riding them on trails.

La monta y los rodeos

Los caballos cuarto de millas son tranquilos. A la gente le gusta montarlos en senderos.

Quarter horses help ranch
workers herd cattle.
The horses can stop and start
quickly to follow the moving cattle.

Los caballos cuarto de milla
ayudan a los trabajadores de
ranchos a arrear el ganado.
Los caballos pueden detenerse
y salir rápido para seguir al
ganado en movimiento.

People ride quarter
horses in rodeos.
These quick horses
race around barrels.

Las personas montan caballos
cuarto de milla en rodeos.
Estos veloces caballos corren
en carreras de barriles.

Quarter horses are gentle
and hardworking.
They are popular horses
for all kinds of riders.

Los caballos cuarto de milla
son mansos y trabajadores.
Son caballos populares para
todos los tipos de jinetes.

Glossary

breed—a certain kind of animal within an animal group

dun—a brown coat color with a dark stripe of hair along the back and darker hair on the legs

foal—a young horse or pony

herd—to round up animals, such as cattle, and keep them together

hindquarter—the part of a horse where the back leg and rump connect to the body

muscular—having strong muscles

rodeo—a contest in which people ride horses and bulls, rope cattle, and race around barrels

sorrel—a light red body color with a lighter mane and tail color

sprinter—a horse that runs very quickly over short distances

Internet Sites

FactHound offers a safe, fun way to find Internet sites related to this book. All of the sites on FactHound have been researched by our staff.

Here's all you do:

Visit *www.facthound.com*

Type in this code: 9781429692243

Glosario

el alazán—un color de cuerpo rojo claro con un color más claro de crin y cola

la alzada—la altura de un caballo

el anca—la parte de un caballo donde la pata trasera y la grupa conectan con el cuerpo

arrear—reunir animales, como el ganado, y mantenerlos juntos

el esprínter—un caballo que corre distancias cortas muy rápido

musculoso—que tiene músculos fuertes

el pardo—un color de pelaje marrón con una franja oscura de pelo a lo largo del lomo y pelo más oscuro en las patas

el potrillo—un caballo o poni joven

la raza—un determinado tipo de animal dentro de un grupo de animales

el rodeo—una competencia en donde la gente monta caballos y toros, enlaza ganado y corre carreras de barriles

la yegua—la hembra del caballo

Sitios de Internet

FactHound brinda una forma segura y divertida de encontrar sitios de Internet relacionados con este libro. Todos los sitios en FactHound han sido investigados por nuestro personal.

Esto es todo lo que tienes que hacer:

Visita *www.facthound.com*

Ingresa este código: 9781429692243

¡Algo súper divertido! Hay proyectos, juegos y mucho más en www.capstonekids.com

Index

Índice

Editorial Credits

Erika L. Shores, editor; Strictly Spanish, translation services; Bobbi J. Wyss, designer; Eric Manske, bilingual book designer; Sarah L. Schuette, photo shoot direction

Photo Credits

Capstone Press/Karon Dubke, 1, 8; TJ Thoraldson Digital Photography, cover, 4, 6, 10, 12, 14, 16, 18, 20

The Capstone Press Photo Studio thanks Rick Brown, Abbey Viessman, Bob Folsom, and Diane Fralish for their help with photo shoots.

Capstone Press thanks Robert Coleman, PhD, associate professor of Equine Extension at the University of Kentucky, Lexington's Department of Animal Sciences, for reviewing this book.